End of Earth

A Collaboration of Poetry and Painting

Poetry by Nolcha Fox

Art by Mike Armstrong

End of Earth

ISBN 978-1-962374-34-7 Paperback
ISBN 978-1-962374-35-4 eBook

Published by Prolific Pulse Press LLC
Raleigh, North Carolina USA

December 2024

Cover Art is by Mike Armstrong

Table of Contents

Acknowledgments

Thanks to Mike Armstrong for sharing his artwork for this book. He is a wonderful human being, a talented artist, and I am honored to have known him for over 30 years.

Thanks to these literary magazines for publishing these poems included in this book.

- Five Fleas: “It took me all day”
- Mad Swirl: “Birds walk the streets”
- Medusa’s Kitchen: “Gardening”
- One Sentence Poems: “Fire and Ash”
- Chewers & Masticadores: “Don’t let the light”
- The Writers Club: “Oranges”
- WyoPoets News Oct 2022: “If I can’t overcome”

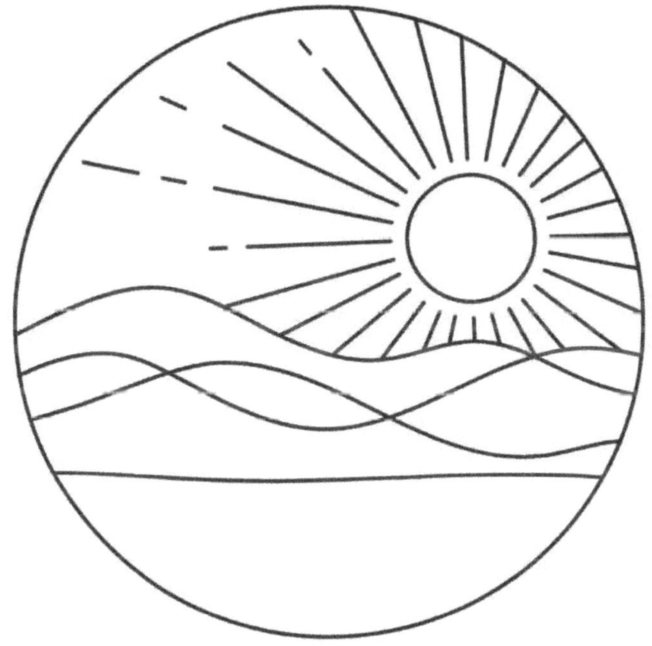

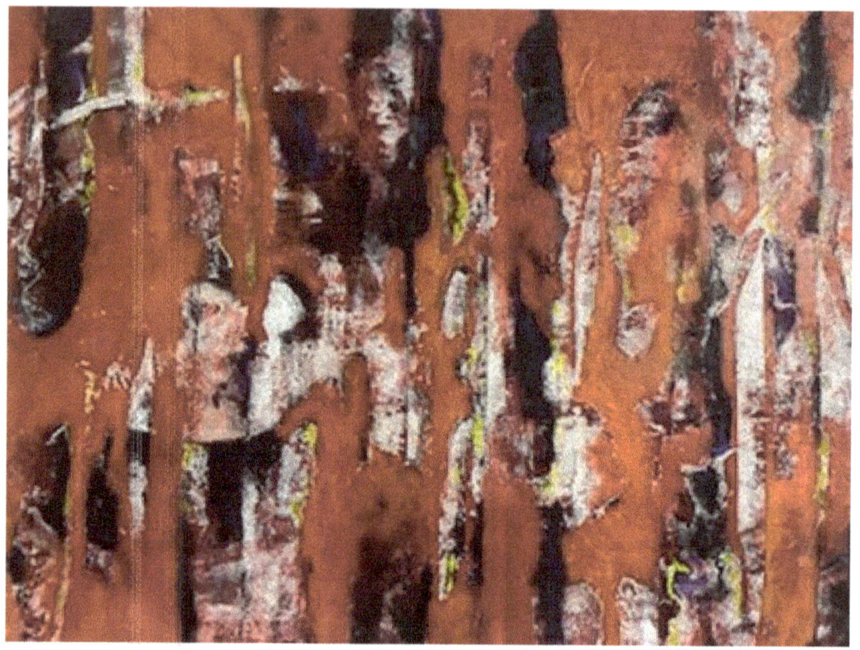

I love children, really, but

they're so unsanitary.
Their clothes are stained
with food and blood.
Snot runs unchecked
down grubby cheeks,
especially when in the pool.
I'll skip the pool and shower.
Thank you.

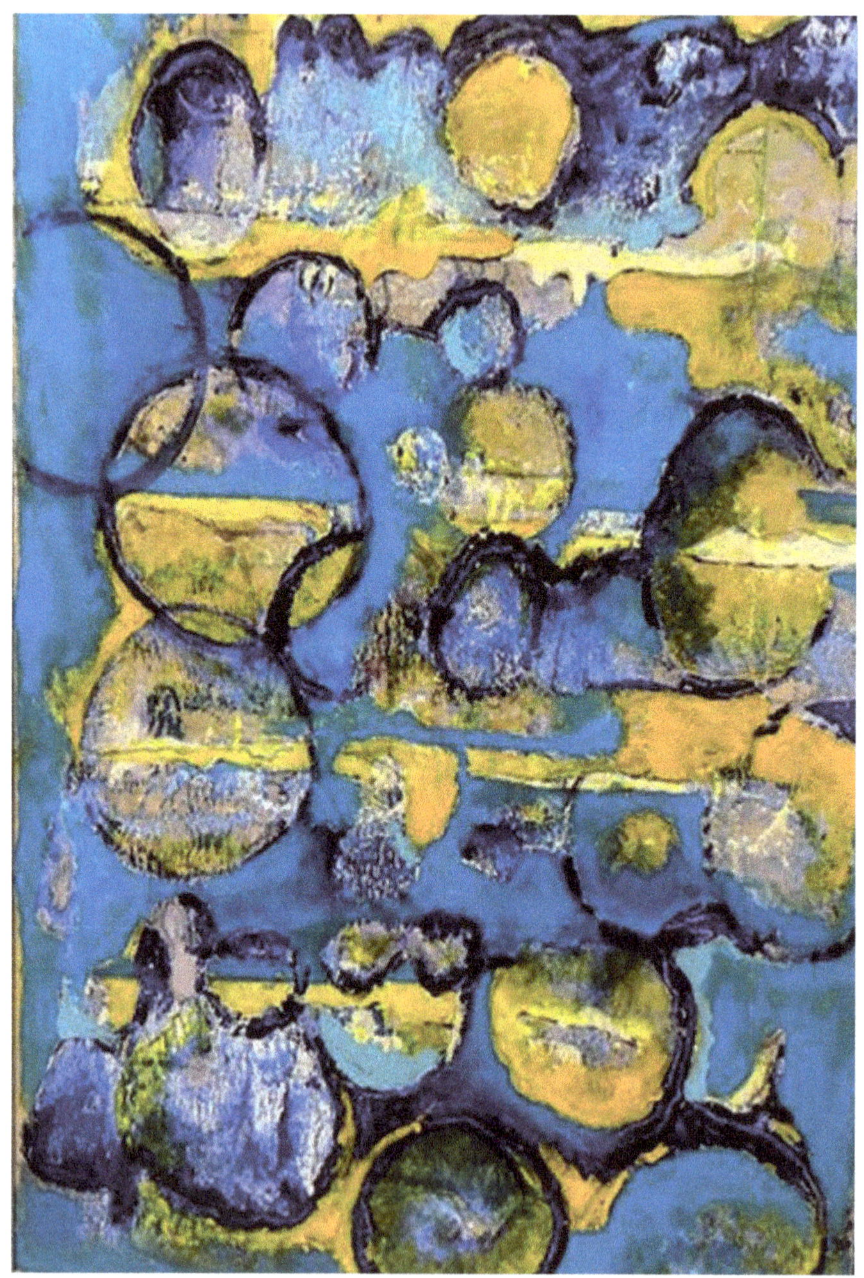

They circle

thinking I taste good,
at first, I think they're vultures.
A second look reveals teeth.
Ah, they are money vampires.
They tell me they can hook me up,
no, cook me up in style.
They see me as some roadkill
and they're a spatula.

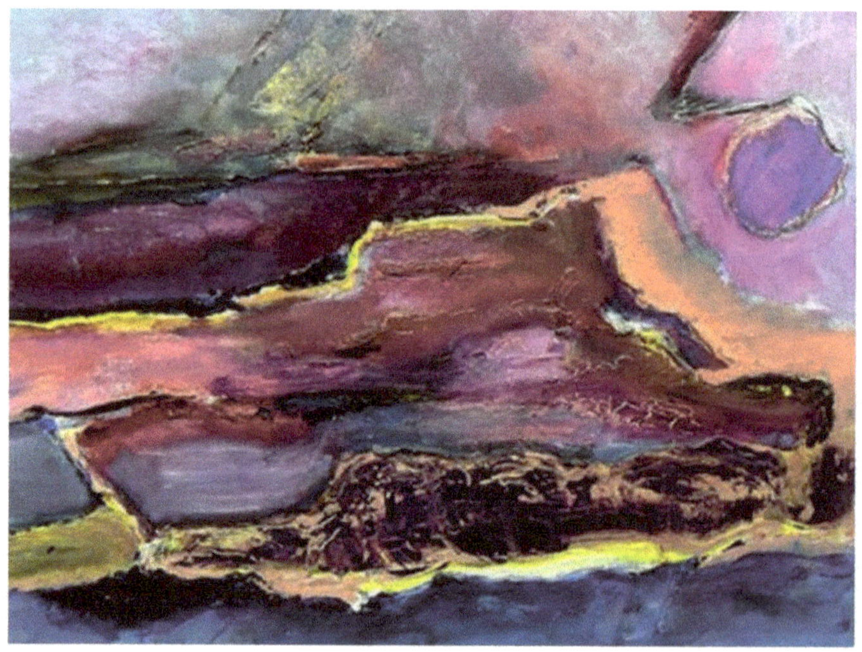

My poems are so

tired, words fall
into clichés
instead of PJs,
drag themselves
into the kitchen
without invitation,
drink my coffee,
and stumble back
to bed, to sleep
on wrinkled sheets.

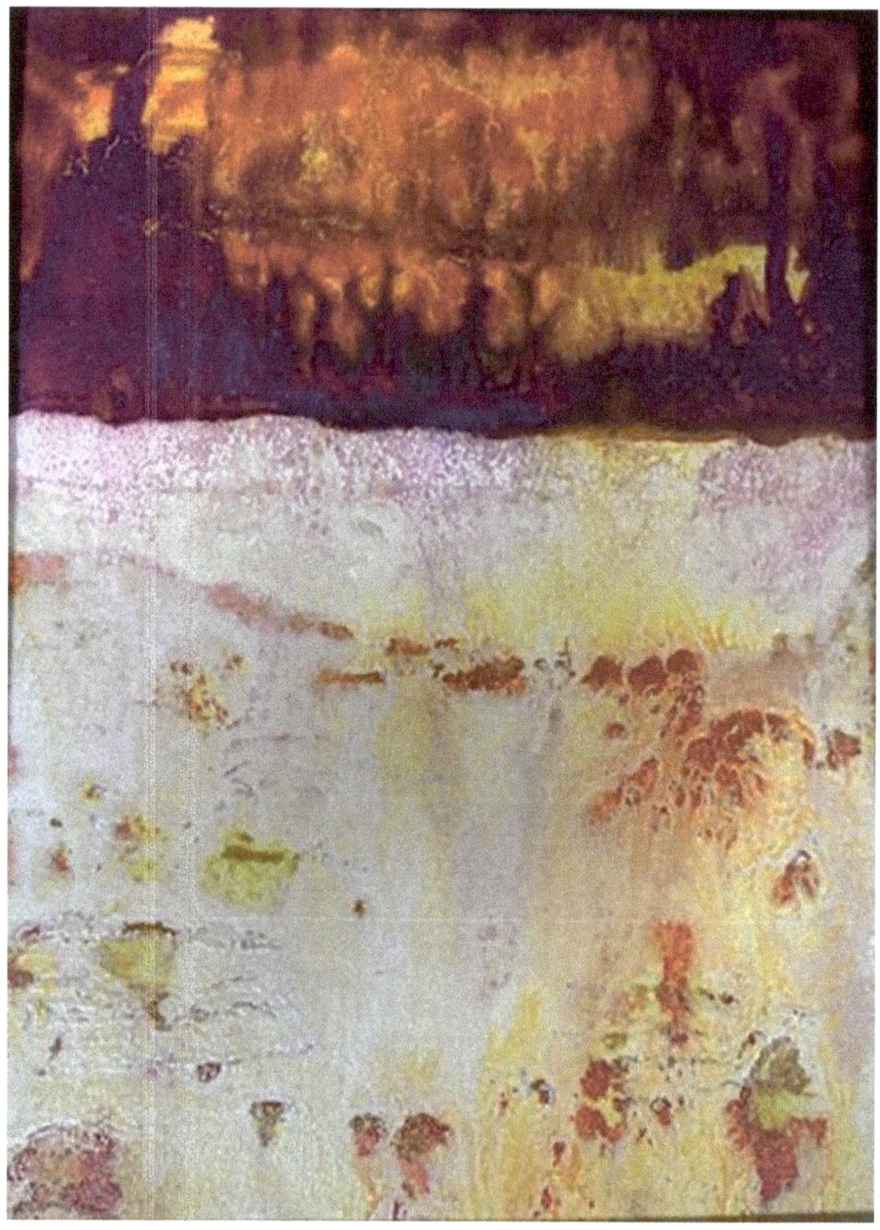

Fire and Ash

This is how we end,
your anger torching paradise,
me erupting, turning earth
to ash.

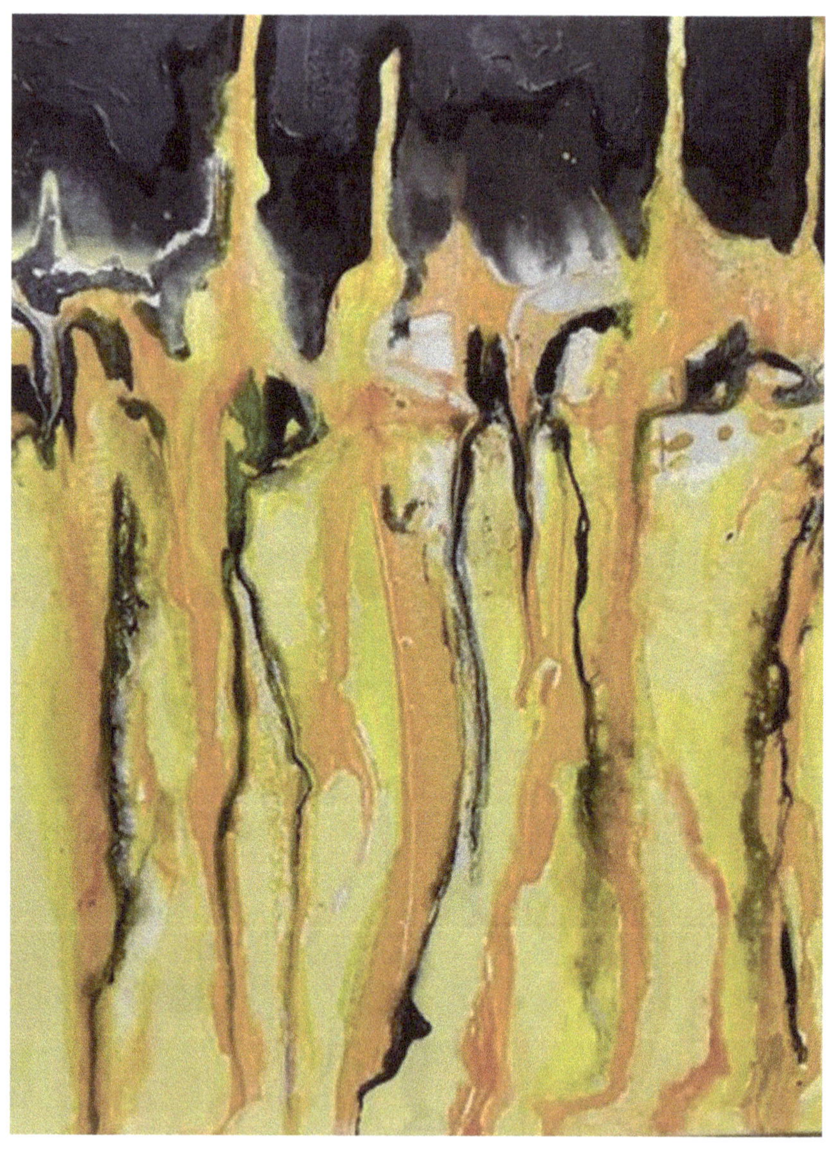

Don’t let the light

seep through the sutures of your skull,
don’t let it set your hair ablaze.
It’s hard enough to fit
into this dark and dreary world
without everybody noticing your fire.

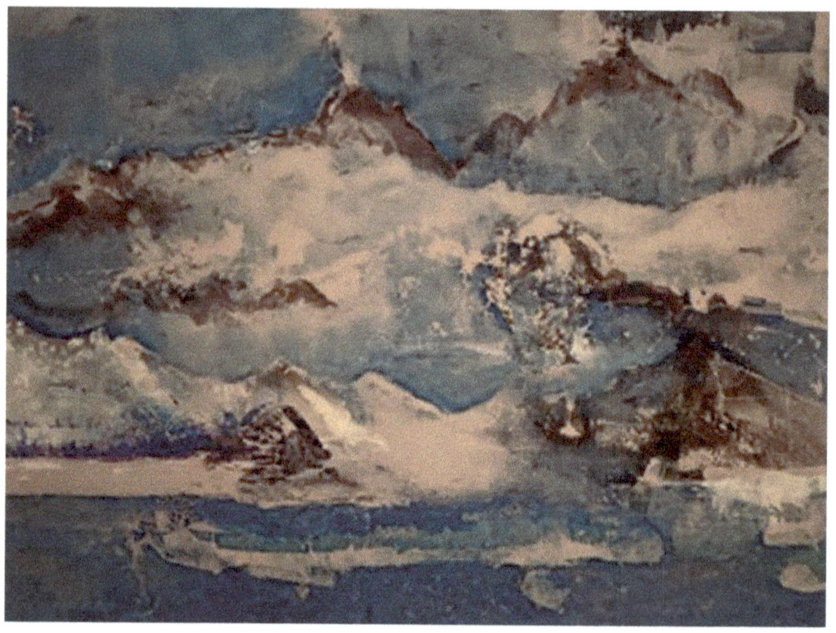

If I can't overcome

the storm, let me be the stillness
that seeps into the clouds
before the rain.
Let me be the pressure drop,
a warning to take shelter.
Let me be the silence
that soothes the branches
just before the wind
announces snow.
Let me breathe in quiet
before the ocean surges.
Let me welcome calmly
whatever comes my way.

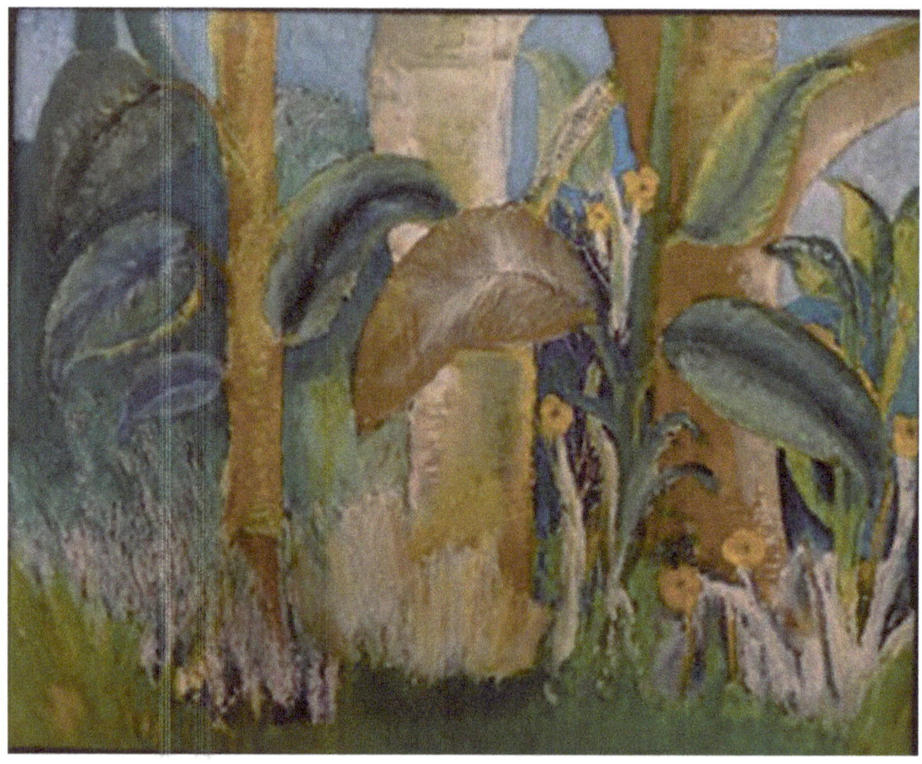

Gardening

She cultivates stupidity in her garden,
planting it with sunflowers and squash.
She tells her friends stupidity
will make them rich and famous.
They buy it from her, every single stalk.

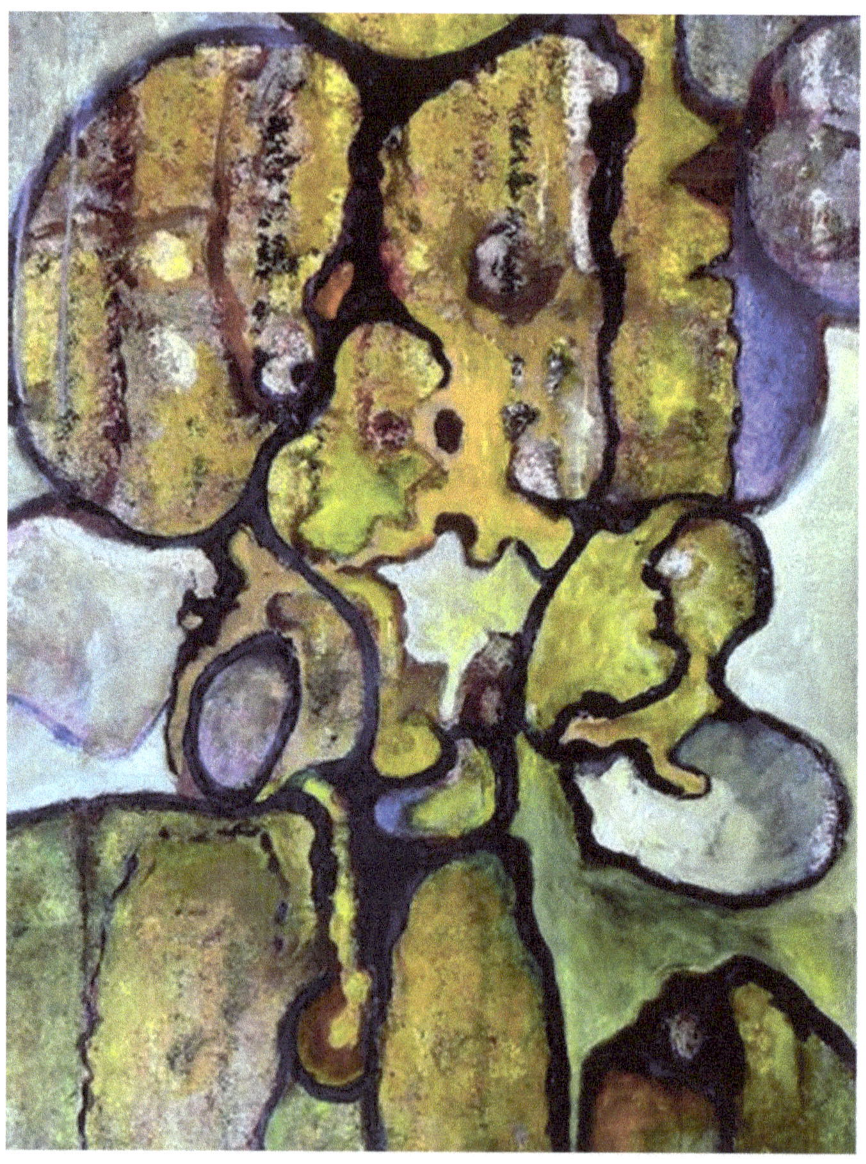

Pieces and Parts

No one sees the whole of me.
Each one grabs a different piece,
a smile, a thought,
a thingamabob.

No one takes my worries.
I stuff them in my chest
where my uncertain habits grow,
a cancer that will leave me dead.

When each one walks
in reverence, following my coffin,
she will mourn the part she knows.
I'll go to ground in pieces.

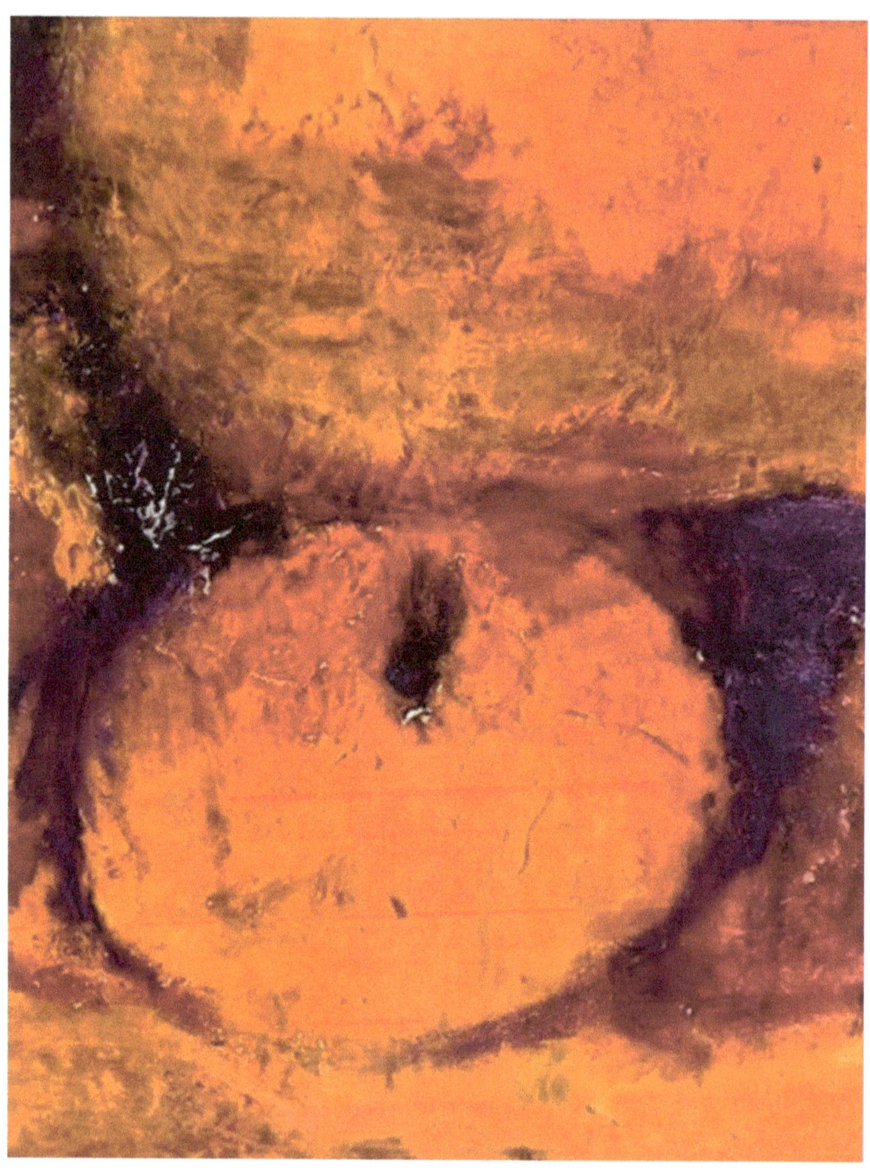

Days melted

into summer's heat,
my bare feet dancing
on the concrete.

Icy theater was my refuge,
cartoon and a double feature,
I cooled my toes and hid in darkness.

Smog-smeared sunsets vanished
into cricket-calling night.
Early bedtime, windows open,

wishing I could be outside.

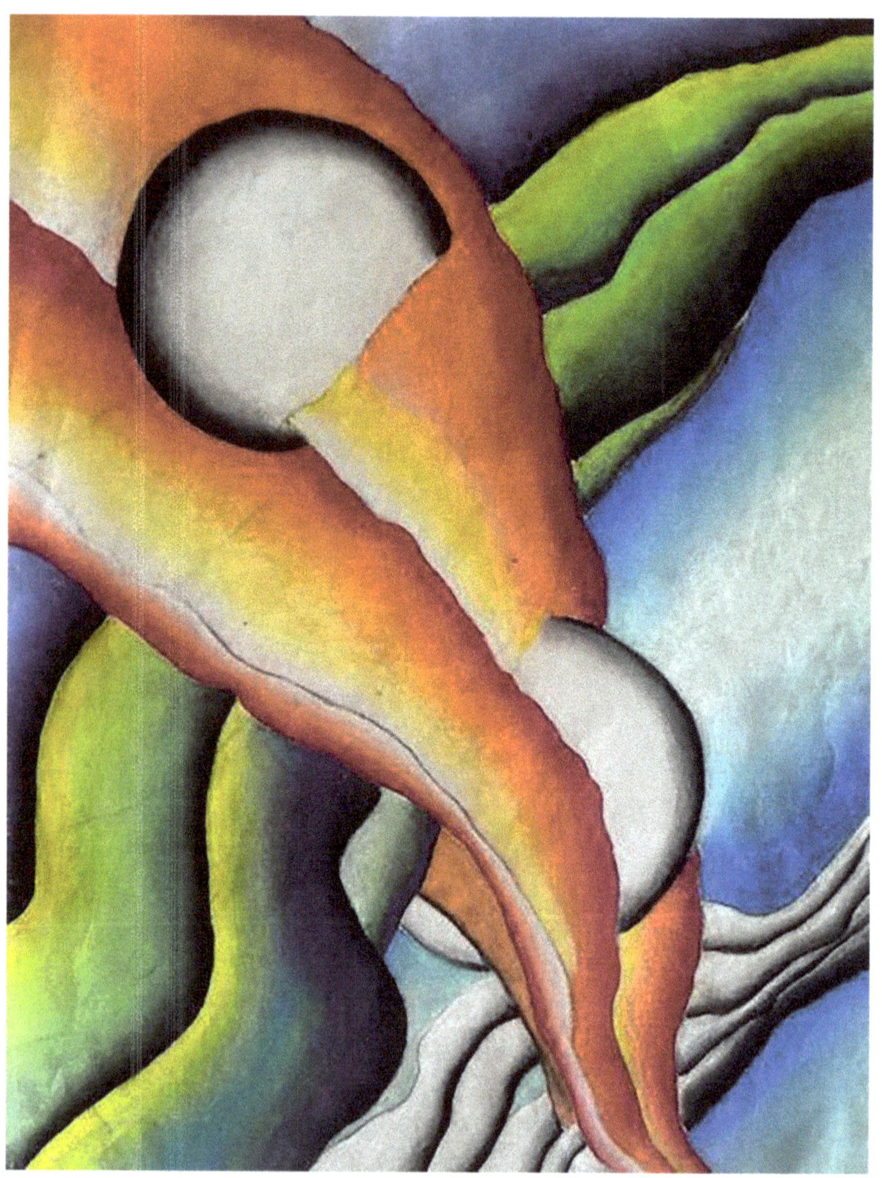

Birds walk the streets

they don't bother with their wings,
fallen angels seeking breadcrumbs
the wind left behind.

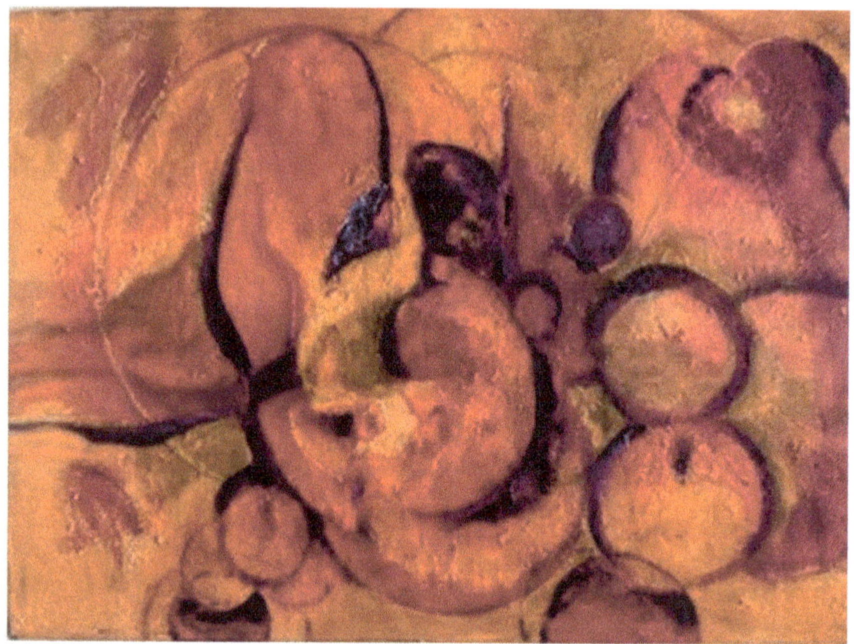

Oranges

for my grandpa

Perhaps the citrus sunset
brought you to my table.
You peeled an orange,
skin all in one piece.
You handed me a naked half.
Eat, you said, eat.
Now you offer sweetness
to wash away my sorrow
that you died before
we shared another orange.

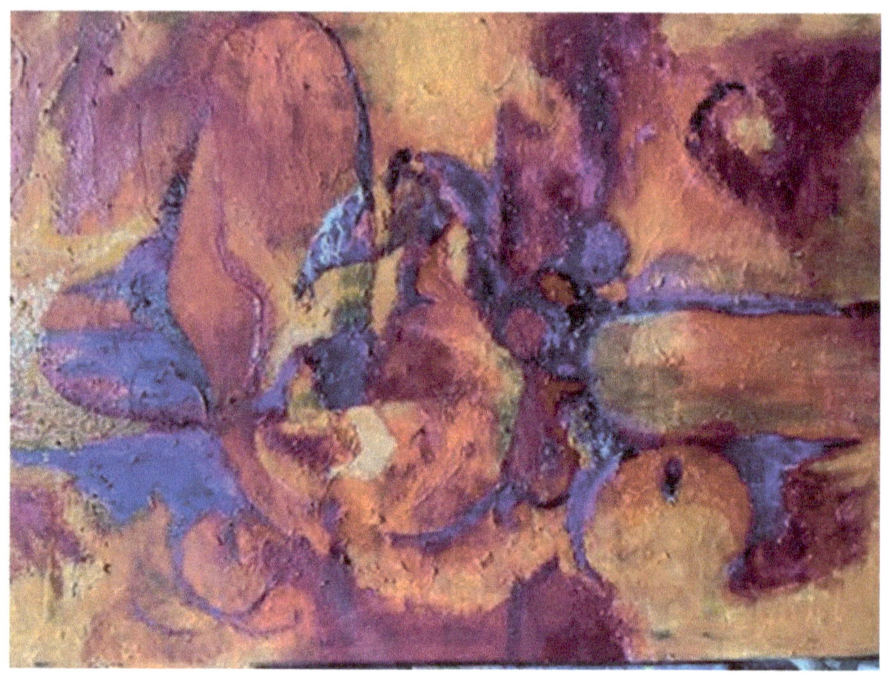

It took me all day

to do nothing.
I could have
stayed in bed
to accomplish
just as much.

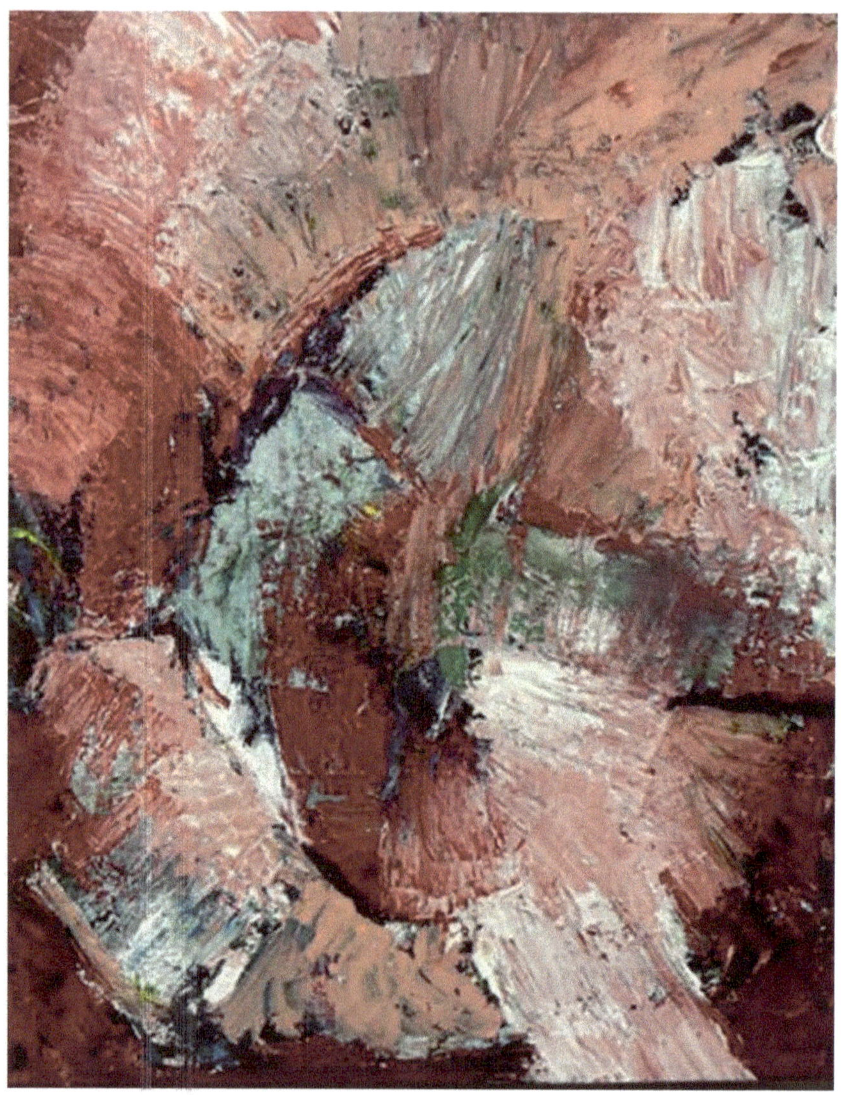

Life wanes

as sun's weak touch
caresses my cold skin.
I barely hear the talk of who
did what to whom
I know I'll leave behind.
The thoughts they cannot utter now
will flower when I'm gone,
while some will keep in lock and key
the harm they think I've done.
My breath slips slowly from my chest,
as slip my thoughts of how I've lived.
I recall as Death stands by

I drank 5,000 cups of coffee.

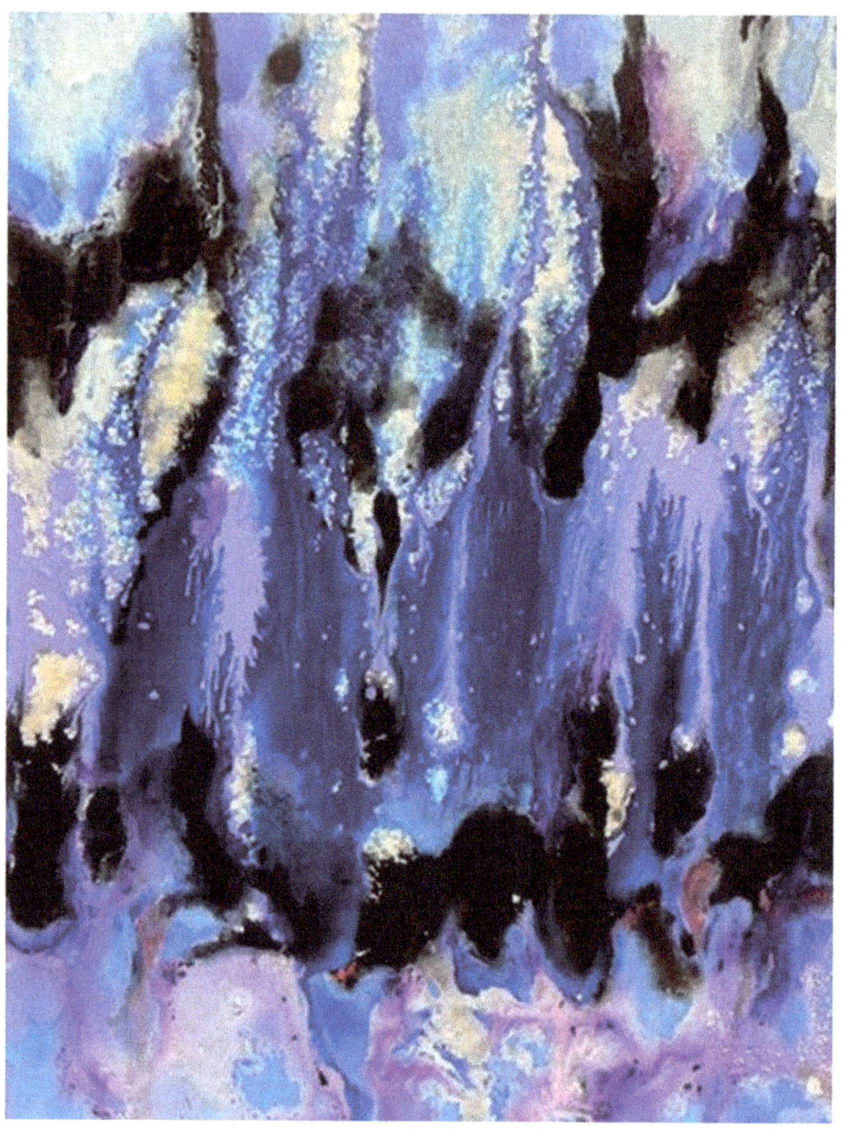

She walked

past the window,
a blur of a shadow,
pacing the tunnels
of his mind.

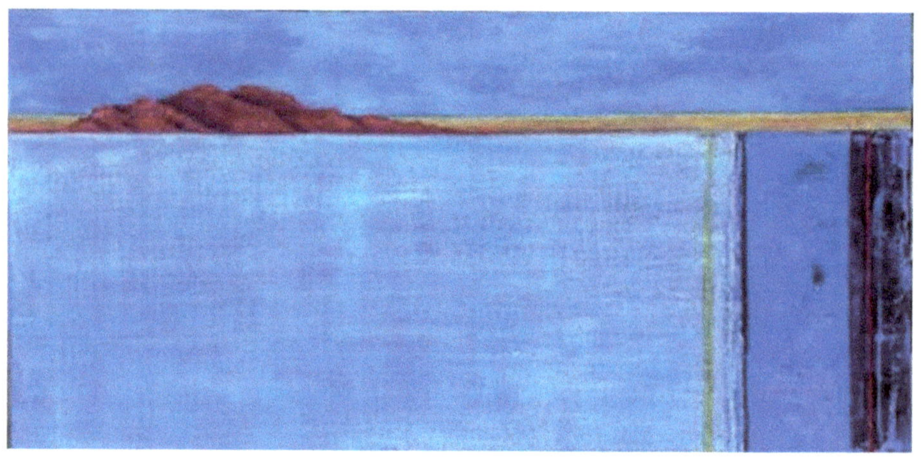

You seem so

still, red mountain,
bordering a silent, placid lake.
What do you hide inside,
how did you rise
and do you guard
the edge of all I know?

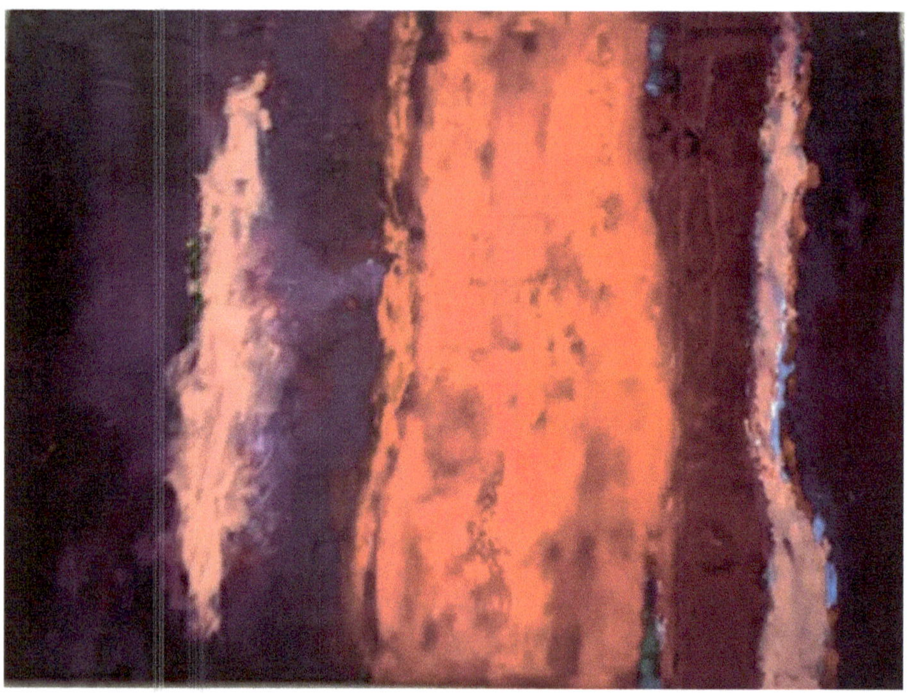

I didn't call

when I missed you.
I thought you'd be there always.
I knew you knew I loved you
even through the silence.
I loved to think of you,
but calling you was painful.
Instead, I held your photograph
imagining you as someone
who you weren't.

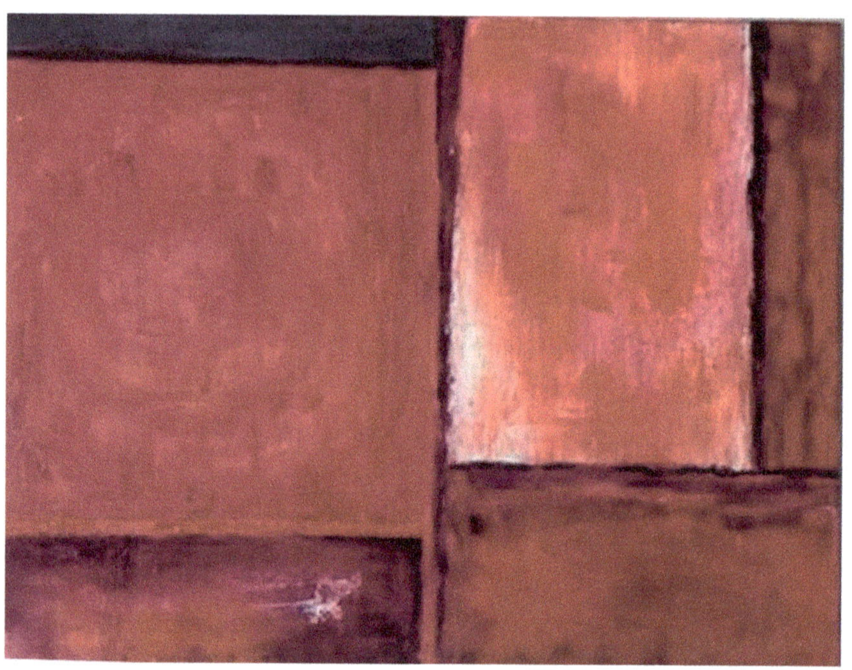

Red

How often you have swaggered past,
your red dress floating in the breeze?
I am just a tiny tick,
a pebble on the sidewalk.
At best I am a mirror
of the things that you disdain.

Every day I leave a poppy,
red, at your front door.
Each flower is a bullet,
I aim it at your heart.
It bounces off your soulless shell,
you crush the petals with your heels.

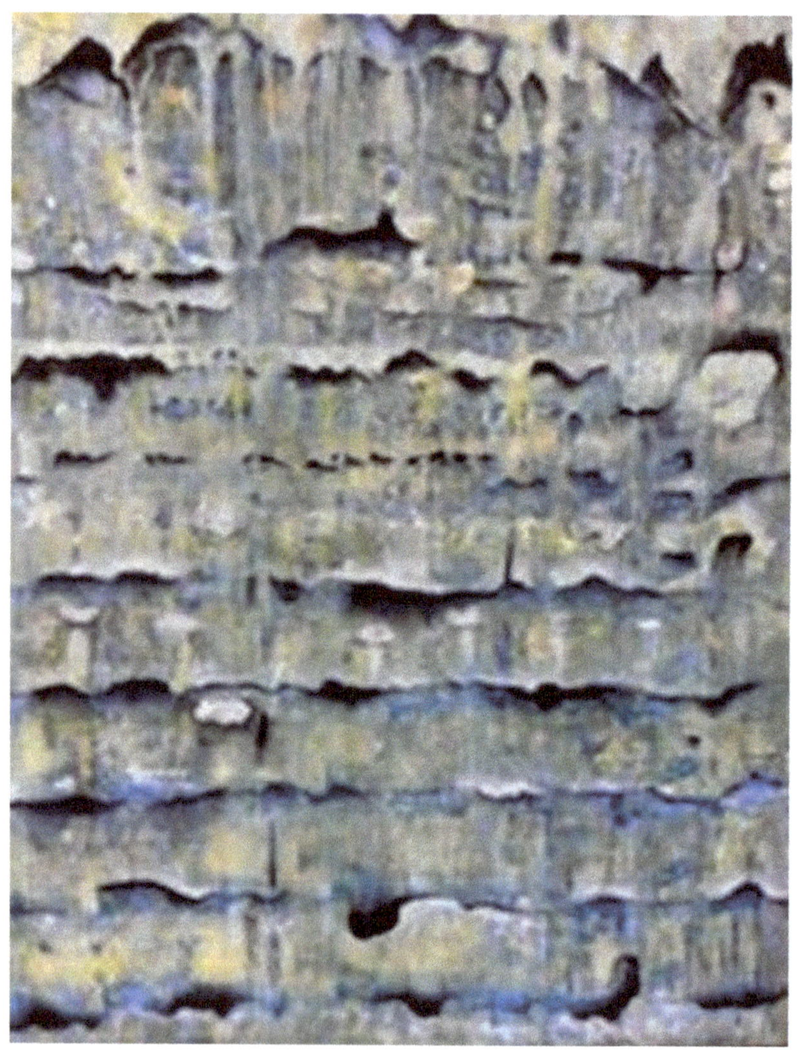

The sun throws

her weight around, lands
on my blizzard-blessed roof.
She's the fat lady,
singing snow into icicles,
hitting sparkling high
notes of glitter and glam.
She kisses the mountains,
then exits stage left.

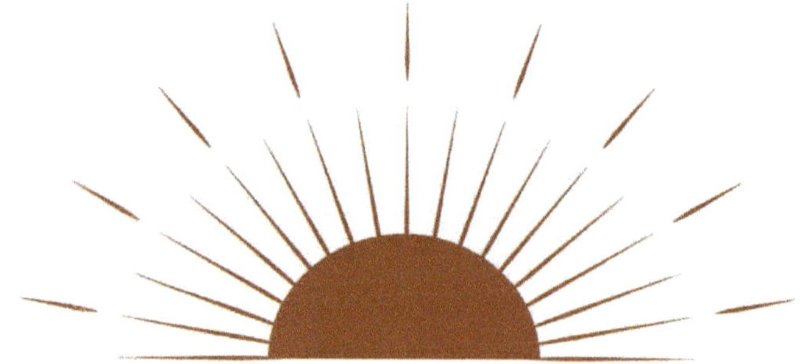

About Nolcha Fox

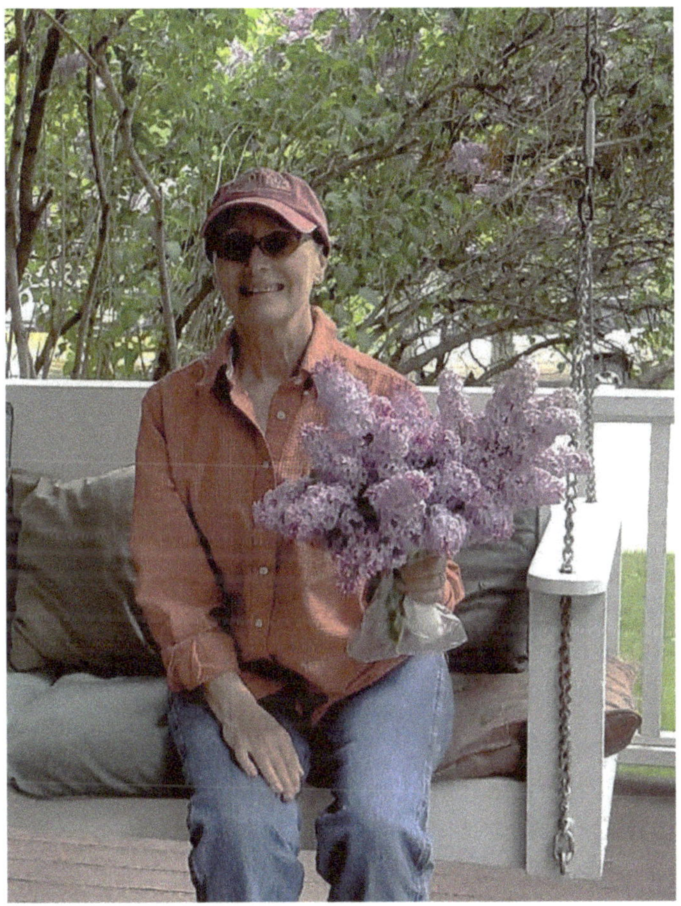

Nolcha Fox's poems have been curated in print and online journals. Her poetry books are available on Amazon and Dancing Girl Press. Nominee for 2023 and 2025 Best of The Net, 2024 Best of the Net Anthology. Nominee for a 2023 Pushcart Prize. Visual Editor for Chewers by Masticadores.

Websites: https://bit.ly/3bT9tYu and
https://nolchafox2.wixsite.com/nolcha-s-written-wor/blog
LinkedIn: https://www.linkedin.com/in/nolchafox/
Facebook: https://www.facebook.com/nolcha.fox/
Medium: @nolchafox_14571

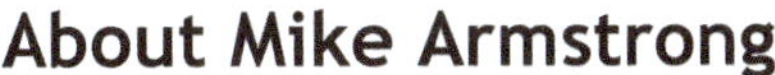

About Mike Armstrong

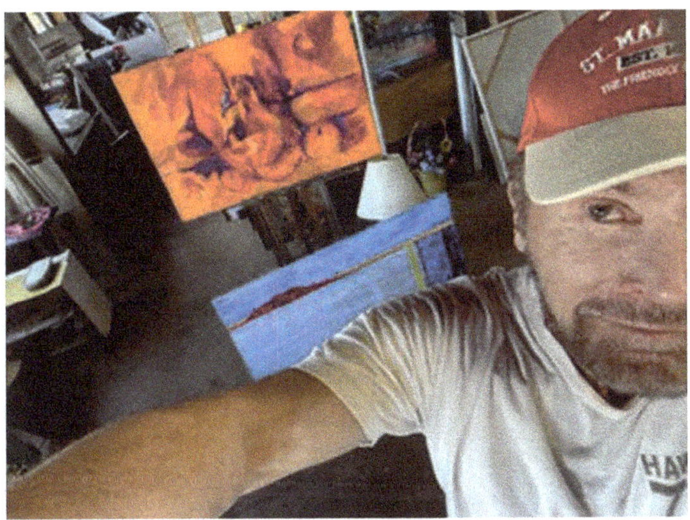

Mike was drawn to art in 3rd grade. He noticed a crayon landscape book report cover displayed in Mrs. Montgomery's English class. Only later did he realize that the artist was his 8th-grade sister, Carol. He also made his first attempt at throwing a pot on the potter's wheel. Actually, it was a small hole in a big piece of clay.

In high school, to stay out of trouble, he spent much of his time in the art room as an art major and art minor.

His time at the University of Alabama as an accounting major was short-lived. He changed to a major in painting and a minor in ceramics.

He was an art teacher for 34 years.
He continues to practice his love of painting and ceramics.

www.ingramcontent.com/pod-product-compliance
Lightning Source LLC
Chambersburg PA
CBHW050019040726
47599CB00014B/1467

9781962374347